MUSLIM HOLIDAYS

by Faith Winchester

Consultant:
Shabbir Mansuri, Director
Council on Islamic Education

Bridgestone Books
an imprint of Capstone Press
Mankato, Minnesota

Fast Facts
- About 1 billion people are Muslims.
- Indonesia has the world's largest Muslim population.
- More than 6 million Muslims live in North America.
- The first masjid in the United States was built in 1915 in Maine.

Bridgestone Books are published by Capstone Press
151 Good Counsel Drive, P.O. Box 669, Mankato, Minnesota 56002
www.capstonepress.com

Library of Congress Cataloging-in-Publication Data
Winchester, Faith.
    Muslim Holidays/by Faith Winchester
    p. cm.--(Read-and-discover ethnic holidays)
    Includes bibliographical references and index.
    Summary: Briefly describes the beliefs of Muslims and eight of the special celebrations that
are a part of the Islamic faith.
    ISBN 1-56065-459-7 (hardcover)
    ISBN 0-7368-4730-8 (paperback)
    1. Holidays—Islamic countries—Juvenile literature. 2. Muslims—Social life and customs—
Juvenile literature. [1. Fasts and feasts—Islam. 2. Islam—Customs and practices. 3. Muslims—
Social life and customs.] I. Title. II. Series.
GT4887.A2W55 1996
394.2'6917671--dc20
                                                                        96-25911

Photo credits
Aramco World Magazine, 6
Dinodia Picture Agency, 18
Photri, cover; Photri/M. Biber, 16
Richard B. Levine, 4
S. Douglass, 20
Unicorn Stock Photos/A. Ramey, 8; Beryl Goldberg, 10
Viesti Associates/Joe Viesti, 14
Woodfin Camp Associates/Robert Azzi, 12

3 4 5 6 05

Table of Contents

The Religion of Islam

Islam is a religion that teaches faith, honesty, modesty, and good deeds. People who follow Islam are Muslims. Muslims call God by the Arabic name Allah.

Islam is based on five practices or acts of worship called pillars. All Muslims accept the following five pillars as the basic acts that they must follow:

Shahadah (shah-HAH-dah)—Declare that there is only one God and that Muhammad is God's messenger.
Salah (sa-LAH)—Perform five regular prayers at set times each day.
Zakah (ZAH-kah)—Pay money to the poor and needy each year.
Sawm (SO-um)—Fast each year during the month called Ramadan.
Hajj (HAAJ)—Travel to Makkah, Saudi Arabia, to perform the holy journey called Hajj. Muslims try to make this journey at least once.

People who follow Islam are Muslims. More than 6 million Muslims live in North America.

About Muslim Holidays

Muslims believe Allah sent many prophets to teach people what He wanted them to do. Muslims honor many prophets such as Noah, Abraham, Moses, and Jesus.

Muslims believe that Muhammad was the last prophet. Muslims wrote the Qur'an as it was told by Muhammad. Muslims believe the Qur'an is a holy book that is Allah's word.

Holidays are important to Muslim communities. Religious holidays teach Muslims the importance of their faith. These holidays also remind people to obey Allah. Other special days help people stay close to family and friends.

Muslims celebrate two important holidays called Eids. Eids are based on the Qur'an and on Muhammad's teachings. Muslims remember important events from Islamic history on other days. Muslim families celebrate weddings and other special days.

Muslim families celebrate weddings.

Jumah

Each Friday, Muslims gather together around midday. They meet in a place of worship called a masjid to pray to Allah. Muslims call this Friday worship service Jumah. This Arabic word means gathering.

In Muslim countries, most people do not go to work or school on Fridays. In other countries, most Muslims perform their usual daily activities on Jumah. But Muslims everywhere try to come together to remember Allah on Jumah. Jumah also is a day to greet other members of the community.

Men, women, and children prepare themselves for going to a masjid on Jumah. They wash their faces, hands, and feet. They wear their best clothes.

Jumah worship lasts about one hour. People say a short prayer of greeting when they enter a masjid. A prayer leader reads from the Qur'an and gives a short speech. Muslims say a prayer together. Muslims believe they will receive blessings for Jumah worship.

Some masajid have a special place for people to wash their hands, faces, and feet before Jumah.

Ramadan

Ramadan is a special time of worship for Muslims. People observe Ramadan during the ninth month of the Islamic lunar calendar. This calendar is based on the cycles of the moon.

Muslims' daily activities are different during Ramadan. Each day begins with a meal before dawn. Muslims fast during the day. They do not eat or drink anything from sunrise to sunset. Only healthy adults must fast during Ramadan. But children often try to fast too. Each night, families gather at sunset. The families eat a meal called iftar.

After iftar, Muslims usually go to the masjid to perform prayers called tarawih. Each night, worshippers read part of the Qur'an. By the end of Ramadan, they have read the entire Qur'an.

Children look forward to Ramadan. Each masjid holds special Ramadan programs for children. They perform plays, recite special poems, and sing songs.

Each masjid holds special Ramadan programs for children.

سورة فاتحة الكتاب

بِسْمِ اللَّهِ الرَّحْمَٰنِ الرَّحِيمِ
الْحَمْدُ لِلَّهِ رَبِّ الْعَالَمِينَ ۝ الرَّحْمَٰنِ الرَّحِيمِ
مَالِكِ يَوْمِ الدِّينِ ۝ إِيَّاكَ نَعْبُدُ وَإِيَّاكَ
نَسْتَعِينُ ۝ اهْدِنَا الصِّرَاطَ الْمُسْتَقِيمَ
صِرَاطَ الَّذِينَ أَنْعَمْتَ عَلَيْهِمْ غَيْرِ
الْمَغْضُوبِ عَلَيْهِمْ وَلَا الضَّالِّينَ

وهي سبع آيات

Laylat al-Qadr

Laylat al-Qadr is a special event toward the end of Ramadan. Laylat al-Qadr means "The Night of Power."

Muslims celebrate an important event in the story of Islam on this night. They believe that Muhammad became a prophet on this day more than 1,400 years ago. Each Ramadan, Muhammad went to a mountain cave. He fasted and prayed there. Muslims believe an angel gave the first words of the Qur'an to Muhammad one night. They called this night Laylat al-Qadr.

Muslims perform extra prayers on the last nights of Ramadan. They pray together late into the 23rd, 25th, or 27th nights of the month. No one knows exactly which of these nights is Laylat al-Qadr. Muslims believe that it happened on an odd-numbered night near the end of Ramadan.

Muslims believe Allah will give them great blessings for prayers said on The Night of Power. In their prayers, Muslims thank Allah for the blessing of the Qur'an.

The Qur'an teaches that prayers Muslims say on Laylat al-Qadr are greater than all the prayers said for 1,000 months.

Eid al-Fitr

Eid al-Fitr is the first day after the month of Ramadan. Muslims celebrate this holiday by breaking their month-long fast.

Muslims throughout the world prepare for Eid al-Fitr. They give food and money to the poor. They clean their homes and decorate them with lights. Muslims prepare special sweets and other dishes for family and friends.

Muslims from the entire community gather to celebrate on Eid al-Fitr. They wear their best clothes and perfumes. They attend Eid prayers at the masjid or outdoor places.

After prayers, Muslims visit with family and friends. They congratulate each other on completing the Ramadan fast. Children receive gifts such as candy and money. The community hosts carnival rides, games, and picnics. Children sometimes perform songs and plays they learned during Ramadan.

Muslims from the entire community gather to say prayers on Eid al-Fitr.

The Hajj

The Hajj is an important event for all Muslims. The Hajj is a journey to the holy city of Makkah in Saudi Arabia. All Muslims hope to make the Hajj once.

Muslims wear simple, white clothes as they perform the Hajj. The white clothes show that all Muslims are equal before Allah.

A huge masjid is in the center of Makkah. A small, ancient stone building called the Ka'bah stands inside the masjid. The Qur'an tells how the prophet Abraham built the Ka'bah as a house of worship for Allah. Muslims walk around the Ka'bah seven times when they visit Makkah. Circling the Ka'bah reminds them that Allah is at the center of their lives.

Muslims perform other acts during the Hajj. Some acts help Muslims remember the prophet Abraham and his family. Muslims walk in places where Abraham walked. They pray as he prayed. The Hajj lasts for 10 days.

Muslims walk around the Ka'bah seven times when they make the Hajj.

Eid al-Adha

Eid al-Adha is on the 10th day of the Hajj. This major Islamic celebration is the Feast of the Sacrifice. On Eid al-Adha, Muslims celebrate the end of the Hajj.

The Feast of the Sacrifice reminds Muslims of the story about Abraham and his son Isma'il. God told Abraham to sacrifice Isma'il. Abraham was willing to kill his son to obey God. This pleased God. So God sent an animal for Abraham to sacrifice instead of Isma'il.

Muslims attend Eid prayers on the morning of Eid al-Adha. They put on their best clothes. They gather at the masjid or at outdoor places. The prayer leader gives a short speech. Everyone then greets each other with hugs and kisses.

After prayers, Muslims visit family and friends. Families that have enough money sacrifice an animal. The animal's meat is shared equally with family, friends, and the poor.

Everyone greets each other with hugs and kisses after Eid prayers.

Mawlid al-Nabi

Mawlid al-Nabi honors the day the prophet Muhammad was born. Muslims try to live their lives by following Muhammad's example.

Mawlid al-Nabi is on the 12th day of the third month of the Islamic calendar. Mawlid al-Nabi is not an official religious holiday. People around the world celebrate Mawlid al-Nabi differently.

Some Muslims study Muhammad's life on Mawlid al-Nabi. They read his teachings.

Some Muslims gather to celebrate Mawlid al-Nabi. They may have dinners or parties to honor the prophet's birthday. Some communities have parades or carnivals.

These Arabic letters mean "Muhammad, the Messenger of Allah."

Hands On: Make a Lantern

Many children make lanterns to celebrate Ramadan. They often carry the lanterns in parades to greet Ramadan's coming. You can make a Ramadan lantern.

What You Need

One small paper sack   Tape
Two pieces of white paper   Scissors
Markers or crayons   Flashlight

What You Do

1. Fold the paper sack so it is flat. Cut a hole in the middle of the sack. You should cut through both layers of paper. Open the sack. The sack now has two windows.
2. Each piece of white paper should be a little larger than the windows of the sack. Color the white paper with markers or crayons. Make pictures or patterns.
3. Tape the white paper inside the bag. Make sure the pictures show in the windows.
4. Gather the opening of the bag around the top of the flashlight handle. Place tape around the bag and handle.
5. Turn on the flashlight. The light will shine through the white paper.

Words to Know

Allah (ah-LAH)—the Islamic name for God

iftar (if-TAR)—a sunset supper during the month of Ramadan

Islam (is-LAHM)—a religion and way of life based on the word of Allah

Ka'bah (KAH-buh)—an ancient house of worship in Makkah, Saudi Arabia; Muslims believe the prophet Abraham built the Ka'bah to worship God.

lunar (LOO-nur)—having to do with the moon

masjid (MAS-jid)—a Muslim house of worship

Muslim (MUSS-lim)—a follower of Islam

prophet (PROF-it)—a person who speaks for God

Qur'an (qur-AHN)—the holy book of Islam

Read More

Aggarwal, Manju. *I Am a Muslim.* My Heritage. New York: Franklin Watts, 1985.

Ahsan, M. M. *Muslim Festivals.* Holidays and Festivals. Vero Beach, Fla.: Rourke, 1987.

Ghazi, Suhaib Hamid. *Ramadan.* New York: Holiday House, 1996.

Useful Addresses

Council on American-Islamic Relations
1050 17th Street NW
Suite 490
Washington, DC 20036

Council on Islamic Education
P.O. Box 20186
Fountain Valley, CA 92728-0186

Internet Sites

About Islam and Muslims
http://www.unn.ac.uk/societies/islamic
Council on American-Islamic Relations
http://www.cair-net.org
Council on Islamic Education
http://www.cie.org
Islamic and Arabic Arts and Architecture
http://islamicart.com
IslamiCity
http://www.islamic.org/default.htm

Index